Bridging the His
Moorish and

BLACK
A
MOOR

BY: COZMO EL

CHAPTER 1

WHAT IS A BLACKAMOOR? (WORD ORIGIN)

What exactly is a blackamoor? The black seems obvious but what of the Moor in this forgotten compound word which was of great use long not so long ago? More importantly, why should anyone care about it's definition?

This word is of enormous significance when it comes to the identity of the population of ex-slaves in the Americas and the world over. There are those in the so-called conscious community that go to great lengths to discredit Moorish perspectives on the history an identity of the descendants of ex-slaves in the United States.

The information in this writing aims to aid those interested in the subject with sound historical facts whereby one may derive a coherent understanding of the usage of the term Moor and it's relation to the people known as "black" today.

There are numerous books written on the word Moor so we shall not run the risk of sounding redundant or repetitive, we shall include only a necessary small section of the classic definition and instead seek highlight the concrete connections between past and present word Moor and also the people.

We shall begin by citing some common dictionaries and the various wordings when it comes to the definition of the word Moor and then review some not so common definitions. Being that online dictionaries are most readily available these days we shall start there.

Wiktionary provides a basic sound definitions of the word which most so-called black people have never heard of but has been in use longer than the term black as referring to a person's identity.

"**Noun**
blackamoor (*plural* blackamoors)

1. (archaic, offensive) A person with dark skin, especially (but not necessarily) one from northern Africa
2. a blackamoor slave, a blackamoor servant; and hence any slave, servant, inferior, or child
3. (heraldry) a stylized Negro Argent, three **blackamoors**' heads couped sable, capped or, fretty gules.

Synonyms

- black
- Negro "(2)

Dictionary.com offers an expanded definition which though lengthly, we shall quote the whole of it. for emphasis and convenience to the reader, we will make bold certain parts of the following excerpt.

"[blak-uh-moo r]

- Word Origin

noun, Older Use: Disparaging and Offensive.
1.
a contemptuous term used to refer to a black person.

2.
a contemptuous term used to refer to any **dark-skinned person.**
Origin of blackamoor

1540-1550
1540-50; unexplained variant of phrase black Moor
Usage note
So-called blackamoors, or black Moors, were **originally black people from North Africa** who worked as servants and slaves in wealthy European households. **The negative connotation of the term comes from its historical association with servitude and from the perception that black Moors were strangely exotic. In 1596, Queen Elizabeth I targeted them for deportation."**

Dictionary.com Unabridged
Based on the Random House Dictionary, © Random House, Inc. 2016.

As we can see, the latter quote offers some etymological information and a bit of historical context. Dictionary.com also provided further historical examples of it's usage and the names of those who used them.

"Examples from the Web for blackamoor

Historical Examples:

"You ought to get one studded with diamonds at that price," laughed Aladdin, and then just for a joke he turned to the *blackamoor*.
Jack and the Check Book John Kendrick Bangs

Six years, and you have turned from **a white-skinned Irishman into a** *blackamoor* !

Paddy Finn W. H. G. Kingston

I've no right to complain, if you will go spending a fortune to **whitewash the *blackamoor*** !
The Adventures of Harry Richmond, Complete George Meredith

"But somebody did try to **wash a *blackamoor* white**," said Bob.
Middy and Ensign G. Manville Fenn

Waiting upon her at either hand were the ***blackamoor* and the negress**.
Heralds of Empire Agnes C. Laut

They think it a beauty, and say **white teeth are the sign of a *blackamoor***.
Devereux, Complete Edward Bulwer-Lytton." (3)

Summarizes:

a.) A person with dark skin, especially (but not necessarily) one from northern
Africa.
b.) A contemptuous term used to refer to any **dark-skinned person.** Keep in mind that the "**The negative connotation of the term comes from its historical association with servitude...**"
c.) (heraldry) a stylized Negro Argent, three **blackamoors'** heads

But what is a Blackamoor? Well the online etymological dictionary makes it quite simple. "**1540s, from Black (adj.) + Moor** with connected element.," http://www.etymonline.com/index.php?term=blackamoor&allowed_in_frame=0

Etymological definition of Black as referring to a person:

"Old English blæc "the color black," also "ink," from noun use of black (adj.). From late 14c. as "dark spot in the pupil of the eye." **The meaning "black person, African" is from 1620s (perhaps late 13c., and blackamoor is from 1540s).** To be in the black (1922) is from the accounting practice of recording credits and balances in black ink.," Ibid

We must note two things with this definition of black. 1.) Black as referring to a person is from 1620. 2.) Blackamoor is perhaps from 1540 which would mean that Black came after Blackamoor etymologically speaking.

What is a Moor?

It is important to know exactly what a Moor is in order to under stand blackamoor. So we will give in brief its definition.
Many people believe that Moor simply means "black." If this was the case then it seems that there would be no reason to place another "black" in front of it making it mean: "black black."

Also, Moor was added to black and not the other way around which would be quite redundant if Moor simply meant black already. Therefore Moor must have meant something different than black.

As we read earlier, black as a distinction for a person begins in 1620, well after blackamoor. Black as an official term for ex slave in the U.S. occurs in the 60s replacing Negro.* The word Moor is of ancient origin. Most European educational curriculums trace this word back to Greece and assign it the definition of black which is why the erroneous definition is prevalent. However, the etymological circles are not so bold and even the etymological online dictionary will not make this claim. They will at least say that perhaps it enters into the Greek language from the native north African word.

"North African, Berber," late 14c., from Old French More, from

Medieval Latin Morus, from Latin Maurus "inhabitant of Mauritania" (northwest Africa, a region now corresponding to northern Algeria and Morocco), from Greek Mauros, perhaps a native name, or else cognate with Mauros "black" **(but this adjective only appears in late Greek and may as well be from the people's name as the reverse). Being a dark people in relation to Europeans,** their name in the Middle Ages was a synonym for "Negro;" **later (16c.-17c.) used indiscriminately of Muslims (Persians, Arabs, etc.) but especially those in India."**

Before we discuss the native name, notice that in the 16c.-17c. it (Moor) became used "indiscriminately for Muslim Persians, Arabs and Indians. This is why there is much confusion in regard to the definition of Moor.

Later the definition of Moor was changes to Arab-Berber which is the common definition used today, if you were to consult a basic dictionary. However, even this definition was changed in the late 70s.

"Otherwise, most of the Moor population speak Berber languages. Islamisation and Arabisation of the population have meant that much of this population have lost all ties with this world. In 1978, even the term *Arabo-Berber* to designate the Moors was replaced by *Arab*." World Public Library sourced from the World Heritage Encyclopedia. http://www.zunelibrary.net/articles/Languages_of_Mauritania

The term Arab itself can be confusing an calls up diverse definition according to the historical knowledge and adeptness of the person using the term.

"This transformation of Arab identity and tradition has been a continuing process for over 1,300 years. Pre-Islamic poetry indicates that in the year 600 "Arab" referred to the Semitic-speaking tribes of the Arabian Peninsula. Quranic usage and other Arabian sources suggest that the word referred primarily to the pastoral Bedouin tribes of the region. Even though camel-herding pastoral nomads were only a minority during Mohammed's lifetime, it seems clear that Arabs were an important social and political force. Their rich oral literature, especially their poetry, and their rejection of authoritarian political forms presented a powerful cultural ideal. Nevertheless, townspeople and others often used the term "Arab" in a pejorative sense. Southern Arabians, both farmers and urban residents, probably did not at first regard themselves as Arab. They probably only adopted this identity when there were political and economic advantages to doing so after the adoption of Islam." http://www.encyclopedia.com/topic/Arabs.aspx

However, in the early Islamic period Arab took on a quite different connotation. It would seem that this connotation has projected itself into modern times but in an extreme form known as Arab Zionism (Modern Arabism) otherwise termed Islamization. Though some would argue this point and though the two are different, it is often difficult to tell the difference.

"The early Islamic period was a time when Arab identity meant that one belonged to an all-encompassing patrilineal descent system. Membership in an Arab descent group brought recognition, honor, and certain privileges, such as exemption from some taxes. **The significance attributed to one s genealogical ties has not prevented Arab societies from assimilating non-Arabs into Arab society, a practice that has remained important throughout Arab history. In the first years after the Arab conquest, it was common to convert to Islam and become an Arab at the same time by forming a relationship with an Arab tribe.** Later, converting to Islam and acquiring Arab identity became separate processes. Islamization continued, but it was no longer tied to Arabization." Ibid

A Clear Definition

The word Moor, mostly understood to be associated with Morocco

actually has its origin in Mauritania which at that time included the geographical area known as Morocco today.
"The English name "Morocco" originates from the Spanish name "Marruecos" which comes from the native Amazigh "Marrakesh," From "Mur = land Akush + of God." *Nanjira, Daniel Don (2010).* African Foreign Policy and Diplomacy From Antiquity to the 21st Century.

Moor is actually derived form a native name of one of the tribes and later kingdoms of Ancient Africa. " The name *Moors* derives from the ancient tribe of the Maure and their kingdom Mauretania." New World Encyclopedia http://www.newworldencyclopedia.org/entry/Moors

More on Blackamoor

Blackamoor, though no longer in use, was a common way of referring to so-called blacks and was prevalent up until the 20th century and can be found to be used in several newspaper, magazines and other media through out the U.S. and the world. Some of these clippings are quite telling.

The distinction "Black." seems to come from an insatiable need to create color distinctions among Moors. This because of the necessary color caste system used during the European domination and colonization of the Moors, who once ruled Africa, Asia and Europe, later becaming the slave population of Europeans.

Tanny (sometimes called white) or Tawny Moors was another distinction used to denote an tan or light brown Moor but this is a "race" based European concept, as a Moor is a Moor regardless of complexion.

see next page...

NATIONAL NICKNAMES.

Terms That Have Come to Be Commonly Applied.

(Notes and Queries.)

Blackamoor, a negro, in contradistinction to a "tawny" or "tanny" Moor. The two divisions of Africa, north and south of Senegal, were known of old respectively as Mauritia, or the country of the Moors, and Nigritia, the country of the blacks; but all Mahometans, whether black or "tanny," were formerly designated "Moors."—e. g., Othello.

16 Oct 1899 pg. 2 Utah Mon Source: Articles About Moors Part 9 – Collected By: Aljamere Bey

In fact, Many equate Blackamoor with slavery but this is not necessarily the case because blackamoors were servants and slaves but also this term was used when referring to any Moor of dark hue (dark in relation to Europeans) irregardless of completion. Likewise, blackamoor predates the official Atlantic slave trade while Moor itself can be traced back to ancient times.

Dolce & Gabbana defend their usage of the blackamoor symbol in fashion

Victor Virgile/Getty Images; Herbert Gehr/Getty Images article published 2012Oct. 27 2012 12:10 AM

"Dolce & Gabbana has stated that these motifs are drawn from traditional Sicilian majolica ceramic designs that often featured the head of a black man, or a "Moor." Based on Sicilian folklore surrounding the Moorish invasion of southern Italy more than a millennium ago, the particular sources for the fashion house's current designs are not necessarily grounded in slavery." "The "racist" blackamoor designs stoking Azealia Banks' ire at D&G have roots that predate slavery." By: Adrienne L. Childs

When one thinks of Italy or Sicily being invaded by Moors, one may call up images of The Moorish Moslems of the middle ages but it actually goes back much further.

Though Moor is an ancient term applied to the ancient so-called black, blackamoor and Moor are used interchangeably in some cases. This gives indication that the blackamoor and the ancient Moor are the same people.

BAD CONSEQUENCES FROM A NAME.—Half the people in the Southern States believed that the Vice President elect is a mulatto, because his father was named Africa Hamlin, and this intensifies their hatred to the Republican party. The grandsire of the Vice President elect seemed to have a liking for geographical names, and he christened four of his sons respectively by the names of Europe, Asia, Africa and America. It very properly fell to the lot of Africa to produce this modern Hannibal, but that no more establishes the fact that he is a mulatto, than that the Carthagenian Hannibal was a blackamoor, because he also was an African. Old Eleazor Hamlin did not imagine for a moment that his desire to unite the four quarters of the globe in his family would one day be one of the causes likely to sever the greatest republic on the face of the earth.

19 Jan 1861 pg 2 Public Ledger Pennsylvania- Collected By: Aljamere Bey

Of course, Hannibal was an ancient Moor, an indication given by the name Hannibal itself.

"Given Name HANNIBAL

GENDER: Masculine
USAGE: Ancient Near Eastern (Latinized), History
PRONOUNCED: HAN-i-bəl **(English)**

Meaning & History
Means "grace of Ba'al" from Phoenician *hann* "grace" combined with the name of the god BA'AL." http://www.behindthename.com/name/hannibal

Ba'al is an ancient Moorish deity of the ancient Moabite/Phoenician Civilization which the Moorish civilization rose out of. Indeed the battle between Moors and the Romans goes back thousands of years. The Muari people inherited the Kemetic (Ancient Egyptians) sciences by way of the Phoenicians/Carthaginians who carried with them the Moabite Script and sciences derived form Kemet. (5)

> The Phoenicians and the Carthaginians, who were concerned chiefly with trade, came to Morocco (and to all North Africa) and stayed for more than 1,000 years on the Moroccan coast (1,200 B.C. - 100 A.D.). They set up trading stations to shelter their boats and sell their goods. The Phoenicians were the first to use money instead of the barter system. They also invented the first alphabet. The Punic language, derived from that of the Phoenicians, spread throughout Morocco, as did their beliefs, traditions and civilization. In this way, the Berbers acquired new techniques in agriculture (for the cultivation of wheat, olive-trees, vines, etc.) stock farming, ore extraction and architecture.
>
> After destroying the town of Carthage, which had been founded by the Phoenicians on the shore of the Gulf of Tunis, the Romans occupied the plains in the north of the country.
>
> The reason why they did so is simple: the Romans were jealous of the wealth of Carthage. They therefore declared war on her, and, in the end, settled on her territory.

"Morocco,"Reading Materials for use in teaching about Various Cultures, National Commission of the Kingdom of Morocco for Uneseco http://unesdoc.unesco.org/images 0000/000043/004350EB.pdf

However, the Muari people were also direct beneficiaries of Kemetic culture. Due to the Romans forces closing the Egyptian Mystery Schools in the 600s. It would not be until the Mauri people (Moors) who in rose up in 7.11 A.D.,, from the self same region that the world would see a resurgence of this ancient Kemetic and Phoenician Civilization by way of Islamic Moorish Civilization.

" As such the people of North Africa were the neighbors of the Egyptians, and became the custodians of Egyptian culture, that they spread through considerable portions of Africa, Asia Minor and Europe. During the occupation of Spain, the Moors displayed with considerable credit, the grandeur of african Civilization." G.G.M James "Stolen Legacy." see pg 43-45

The Moorish Empire ruled Spain and various territories from 711A.D. to 1492. The fall of the last stronghold in Granada begins the enslavement of Moors.

Blackamoor Icons

Some become confused and mistake the Blackamoor icons for the Mammy and Sambo (Minstrel) type images which are rooted in the North American Slave society and culture of the United States but as we can see, this is not the case, the Blackamoor symbol predates this history. Likewise, the blackamoor Icons are telling when it comes to the origin of the people from which the slaves were amassed.

On the contrary. Blackamoor pieces are usually quite beautiful and are to be admired by art, antique and luxury and though some may be pot rayed as servants, they are not unflattering in appearance.

However, it was the objective of the European in America to demean the so-called black image in order to justify the grave injustices perpetrated by Eropean Society in the U.S.

"A Blackamoor is not a Jigaboo and More: The Black Portraiture[s] II Conference and ReSignifications Exhibition

"When I first started this research the 'blackamoor' objects, although ubiquitous, languished in museums and antique shops unstudied and given no critical attention. Now, many important and exciting contemporary artists featured in *Resignifications* are responding to these very objects. It is both gratifying to me and illuminating for my research. Their perspectives on the peculiar issues of race, beauty, servitude, and representation raised by the blackamoors open up new interpretive possibilities for objects that are centuries old."(4

Black-a-Moors in the European Imagination II: Beyond Dolce and Gabbana https://pdjeliclark.wordpress.com/

2012/10/27/black-a-moors-in-the-european-imagination-ii-beyond-dolce-and-gabbana/

19th c. Italian, carved of specimen marbles and hardstones as Blackamoors, each wearing a striped turban and antique dress. 32"H. 31"W. Condition: expected light wear, repair to left shoulder of one Moor (lapis brooch), otherwise good.

http://www.antiques.com/classified/Antique-Garden---Architectural/Antique-Statuary/Antique-PAIR-ANTIQUE-ITALIAN-CARVED-VENETIAN-BLACKAMOOR-STATUES

Slaves were not permitted to read and could be killed or tortured for attempting to. Blackamoors were usually depicted in their traditional moorish dress another indications which reveal the identity of those depicted.

Blackamoor Heraldry and Pics

Blackamoor Heraldry or MoorHeads are another piece of art and history that pertains to the so-called blacks and their identity and are in use in art, flags and family crest.

They do not all mean the same thing however, and can range from one extreme to the other:; from slave to Nobility. Many European families deemed it an honor to have Moorish ancestry and thus openly displayed them on their family banners and crest. Others used it as a sign of the domination and defeat of Moors.

"The Moor's head is not rare in European heraldry. It still appears today in the arms of Sardinia and Corsica, as well as in the blazons of various noble families. Italian heraldry, however, usually depicts the Moor wearing a white band around his head instead of a crown, indicating a slave who has been freed; whereas in German heraldry the Moor is shown wearing a crown. The Moor's head is common in the Bavarian tradition and is known as the *caput Ethiopicum* or the Moor of *Freising*" "The Holy See," Coat of Arms of his Holiness Benedict XVI

Coat of Arms of Pope Benedict XVI

Taken from the Book "Nature Knows no Color Line," by J.A. Rogers. Picture shows Various French, Dutch and Belgian Families with so-called blackamoor names

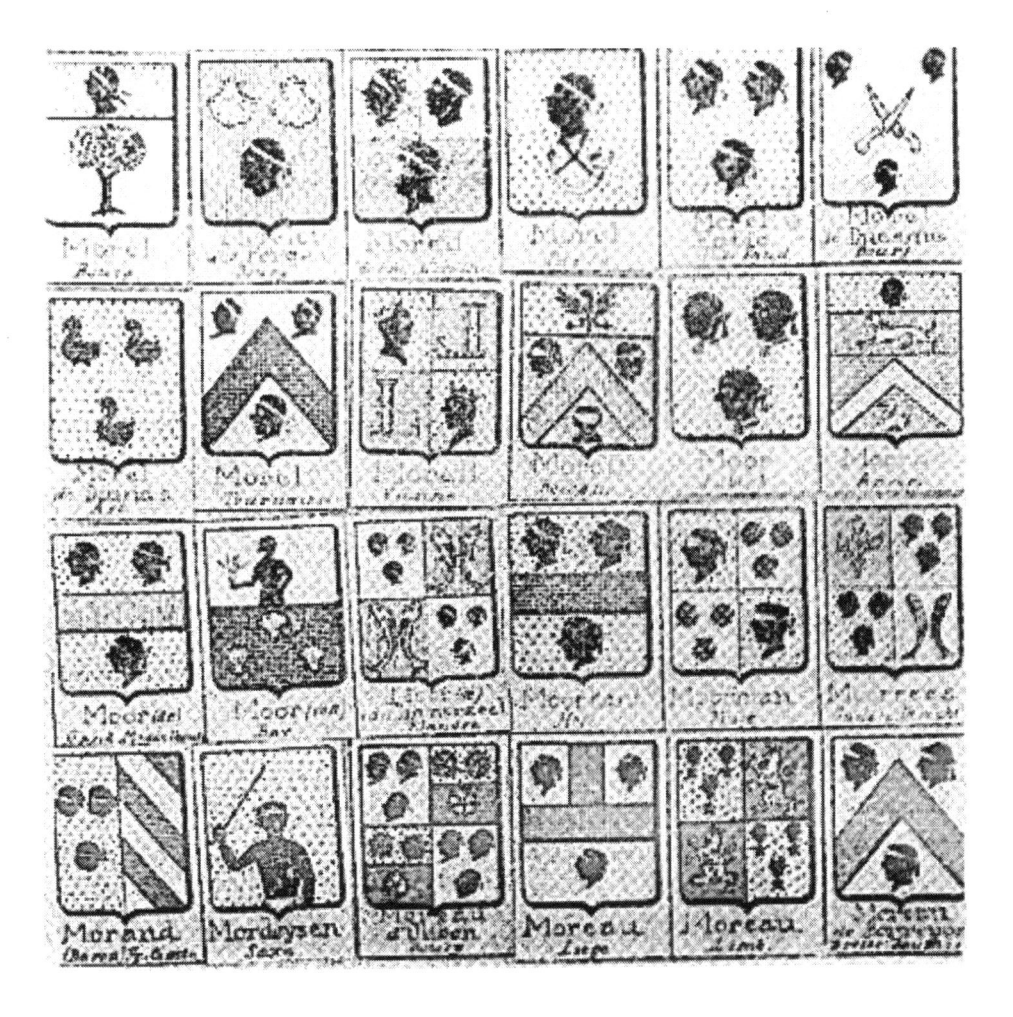

Notice the Moor and it's derivatives

Blackamoor Germany

Clockwork Automaton Cocoa Blackamoor
Store Display Store Window Figure 1900 | eBay

Blackamoor France

Cartier Paris blackamoor head clip
brooch, French, circa 1938.

Blackamoor England

Hardy's Kimberley Brewery Ltd. merged with Hanson's in 1930 to form Hardy's and Hanson's, one of the largest breweries in Nottinghamshire.

Here is an Interesting Blackamoor in Native /Aboriginal Headdress

About 1800-1850 Painted wood
Object number 1919.3.HITW
Given by Councillor JW Thompson, 1919
http://revealinghistories.org.uk/legacies-stereotypes-racism-and-the-civil-rights-movement/objects/blackamoor.html

Ashbourne, Derbyshire, England

"Further along the street stood one of the most important inns, the BLACKAMOORS HEAD, now the site of Wigleys shoe shop, and often shortened to the Black's Head. The name originated from the 16th century perhaps referring to Shakespeare's Othello. A greatly respected inn, at the beginning of the 19th century it was bought by the Landlord of the Green Man and amalgamated on to one site. In its heyday the Blackamoor Inn was used for many important events such as inquisitions, Courts, Archdeacon's Visitations, and in 1748 even the County Assizes were held there." https://www.google.com/search?q=blackamoor+europe&tbm=isch&tbo=u&source=univ&sa=X&ved=0ahUKEwi7qKH-9sDLAhWKLyYKHTtaAxUQsAQIHw&biw=1600&bih=684#imgrc=7LtTtjWb9jV9oM%3A

IDENTITY, A MONUMENTAL DISASTER FOR MELANATED PEOPLES HISTORY

By: Cozmo El

Name the two ways of identifying people?

Answer: By the land they are on and by the language they speak.
What exactly does it mean to **identify?**
Answer:

1. to know and say who someone is or what something is 2. to find out who someone is or what something is
3. to show who someone is or what something is http://www.merriam-webster.com/dictionary/identify

Identifying or knowing who the so-called black people in the United States truly are is a daunting task because so-called blacks are dispossessed of the two components used to identify a people. Namely, land and language. The lack of land possession and language coupled with the restructuring of history and destruction of precious archeological sites by racially motivated governments, has kept a cloud of uncertainty over the vast landscape of the history of melanated peoples of the world. This is especially true in regards to the so-called negro, black and colored populations of the Americas.

There is a very clear example of this occurrence of termed " Cultural Cleansing," by media outlets. However, whose culture is being cleansed?

"Islamist militants in Iraq and Syria continue their war on the region's cultural heritage, attacking archaeological sites with bulldozers and explosives.

The so-called Islamic State (ISIS) released a video that shocked the world last month by showing the fiery destruction of the Temple of Baalshamin, one of the best-preserved ruins at the Syrian site of Palmyra. Last weekend, explosions were reported at another Palmyra temple, dedicated to the ancient god Baal; a United Nation agency says satellite images show that larger temple has largely been destroyed." http:// news.nationalgeographic.com/2015/09/150901-isis-destruction-looting- ancient-sites-iraq-syria-archaeology/

The National Geographic article goes on to list some of the sites that have been looted, damaged or destroyed.

"Ancient Assyria was one of the first true empires, expanding aggressively across the Middle East and controlling a vast stretch of the ancient world between 900 and 600 B.C. The Assyrian kings ruled their realm from a series of capitals in what is today northern Iraq. Nineveh was one of them, flourishing under the Assyrian emperor Sennacherib around 700 B.C. At one point, Nineveh was the largest city in the world." Ibid

Broken statue head of a lamassu , the winged human-headed bull from the Ancient Assyrian palace at Nebi Yunus.

"Nimrud was the first Assyrian capital, founded 3,200 years ago. Its rich decoration reflected the empire's power and wealth. The site was

see next page...

Nineveh. Nebi Yunus. Head of a lamassu at the Iraqi excavation of the entrance to a late Assyrian building east of the mosque. (photo May 1990)

excavated beginning in the 1840s by British archaeologists, who sent dozens of its massive stone sculptures to museums around the world, including New York's Metropolitan Museum of Art and the British Museum in London. Many originals remained in Iraq.."Ibid

Traditional history has limited the inhabitation of melanated people to Africa, but it is clear today that so-called ancient black inhabited various regions of the planet. Likewise, they establish great civilizations in Asia, Africa, India, America, etc. The ancient civilizations of the mesopotamia are no different.

"After deciphering the cuneiform script and researching ancient Mesopotamia for many years Henry Rawlinson (1810-1895) discovered that the founders of the civilization were of Kushite (Cushite) origin... John Baldwin wrote in his book *"PreHistoric Nations"* (1869): "The early colonists of Babylonia were of the same race as the inhabitants of the Upper Nile. "This was corroborated by other scholars including, Chandra Chakaberty, who asserted in his book *"A Study in Hindu Social Polity"* that "based on the statuaries and steles of Babylonia, the Sumerians were "of dark complexion (chocolate colour), short stature, but of sturdy frame, oval face, stout nose, straight hair, full head; they typically resembled the Dravidians, not only in cranium, but almost in all the details." (PreHistoric Nations by John D. Baldwin, New York: Harper & Brothers, 1869, pg. 192) (A Study in Hindu Social Polity by Chandra...

Engraving of Ancient Mesopotamian (Sumerian) Figure's Head

...Chakaberty, Delhi: Mittal Publications, 1987, pg. 33)http:// atlantablackstar.com/2014/04/16/5-ancient-black-civilizations-africa/5

Noble Drew Ali suggest that Cushites were the first to migrate to Africa from the Fertile Crescent bringing a wave of migration which has bering on the identity of so-called blacks in America.

"Old man Cush and his family were the first to inhabit Africa. His and father Ham and his family were the second, then came the word Ethiopia..." Holy Koran Noble Drew Ali

In fact, the oldest skeletal remains in the world have been found in the location described by Drew Ali as being the inhabitation of Cush. "North East and South East Africa and North West and South West Africa was his fathers dominion..."Ibid

Drew Ali also goes on to state: " The Moabites from the land of Moab received permission from the Pharaohs of Egypt they are the founders and the true possessors of the present Moroccan Empire, with their Canaanite, Hittite and Amortie brethren who sojourned from the land of Cannon seeking new homes,"

Noble Drew Ali says: "Brethren," Now brethren can also means groups of diverse parts of society or religious sects but it does not appear that these definitions apply exclusively in this case. Why? Because all the above mentioned groups are descendants of Ham according to Biblical Scholars.

The Hittites were descended from Heth, the son of Canaan (and great-grandson of Noah, Genesis 10:15). A people descended from Emer, the fourth son of Canaan, Genesis 10:16. and Cannanites are descendants of Canaan, the son of Ham whom Biblical Scholars attribute to being the father of the so- called black people of the world.

The Moabites are often attributed to being Shemite or descendants of Shem and thus separated from the Hamites as a distinctly other people.

However, aside from the fact that Ham and Shem are attributed to being the defendants of Noah, making them brothers, The bible also gives indication the Moabites have an even more ancient origin.

"I see him, but not now; I behold him, but not near. A star will come out of Jacob; a scepter will rise out of Israel. He will crush the foreheads of Moab, the skulls of all the people of Sheth." Numbers 24:17
Here we can clearly see that Moab and the people of Seth are one and the same. Seth is the son of Adam placing Moab as decedents of Adam himself. But let us return to Cannan.

"Name of the son of Ham, and a brother of Cush (Ethiopia), Mizriam (Egypt), and Put (Phut), occurring in the geographical-ethnographical table, Gen. ix. and x. Originally the name "Canaan" was not an ethnic term. It belongs primarily to the vocabulary of geography; the curse pronounced upon its bearer for the misconduct of Ham demonstrating only the knowledge of the author that the dominant Semitic population of the land so designated was the deposit of a wave of immigration and conquest coming from the south. Originally an appellative (compare Moore, on the use of the article in Egyptian inscriptions, in "Proceedings of Am. Oriental Soc." 1890, lxvii. *et seq.*), it described some peculiar aspect of the country, and was only later transferred from the territory to the inhabitants. http://www.jewishencyclopedia.com/articles/3955-canaan

Often times and as a result of the destruction of monuments and precious historical relics, crucial history can be lost forever and this is obviously the hope of those who comment such atrocities. It is because of this tactic and others that many so-called black people today do not know of their true origin. Ultimately, making it nearly impossible for them to see the relevancy of acts such as this or at least how it relates to them.

It is as a result of the lack of Identity that many world events that have bearing on so-called black people and their historical Birth Rights and heritage go unnoticed and unrecognized as relating to them. In essences, they are unable to "Identify," themselves and or their relevancy in history (biblical or otherwise) as well as current affairs.

Other Books By Author

Order at: amazon,com

Moor: What They didn't Teach You in Black History Class Paperback – March 7, 2015

by <u>Min. Cozmo El</u> **Paperback** $13.00

Key Points (Key Points Moorish Dvd Transcription): Essays on the Margins of Hidden Moorish History

May 1, 2014
by Min. Cozmo Ali El **Paperback** $12.00

The Cherry Tree and The Hatchet: Was George Washington The Hatchet Man for European Political Will in a Conspiracy...

Jan 26, 2015 by Min. Cozmo El **Paperback** $11.00

Key Points Trilogy: Essays on the Margins of Hidden Moorish History

Jan 26, 2015 by Min. Cozmo El **Paperback** $24.00

Ancient Kemite Islam and the Preservation of Ma'at (Addendum): Plus Information and Illustrations not Included...

Nov 17, 2014 by Min. Cozmo El **Paperback** $6.00

Ancient Kemite Islam and the Preservation of Ma'at: The missing link between Kemetic and Moorish civilization

Apr 22, 2014
by Min. Cozmo Ali El **Paperback** #13.00

Key Points II: Deconstructing the colonization of Moors (Key Points (Essays on the Margins of Hidden Moorish...

Jul 2, 2014

by Min Cozmo Ali El **Paperback** $11.00

Al Munaafiqoon The Dissemblers: A Treatise on the Hypocrite According the the Quran

Sep 29, 2014
by Min Cozmo Ali El **Paperback** $6.00

By Min. Cozmo Ali El Ancient Kemite Islam and the Preservation of Ma'at: The missing link between Kemetic and...

Student Edition $10.00

Order Today!

NEW!

Book Release/Bio

"What They didn't Teach You in Black History Class," Part 1 and 2

Covers interesting facts about Moorish history and articles which bring the information current. This book contains a wide range of topics arranged neatly for easy use along with factual references and internet links for those who like to take their studies to the next level.

Cozmo El is the Minister of Culture of the Far West Province of Moors and Moorish Science Temple 101, California (Califa). The Ministry of Culture of Moors is ministry responsible for maintaining and promoting the culture of Moors.

El is an accomplished author and has written several books on Moorish History and language. Most popular books by Cozmo El included **"Moors What they Didn't teach you in Black history Class I, I and II,"** and **"Key Points Trilogy," Essays on the Margins of Hidden Moorish History,"** a collection of **"Key Points," I, II and III.**

Cozmo El is a member of the Moorish Science Temple and Alpha Mu Gamma, the National Collegiate Foreign Language Honor Society, the first and largest national collegiate foreign language honor society of the United States. Because of his love for language, El has also written the book **"The Moabite Key, Introduction to The Moabite Script: A Phenomenological and Grammatical Approach."**

Cozmo El is a **"... a budding renaissance man." according to** moorishamericannews.com Cozmo El's **"Moors, What They didn't Teach You in Black History Class,"** was listed among

the **"15 Books that all Black people should read,"** allblackmedia.com and blackkpepper.com

As the Minister of Culture, it is El's solemn duty to promote positive programs which, restore, preserve and interpret ancient and modern Moorish Culture and Traditions. To this end, El's efforts are directed toward the rich traditions of writings, poetry, music, art in all it's forms and media.

Citations Note (2) and (3)

blackamoor

/ˈblækəˌmʊə; -ˌmɔː/
noun
1.
(archaic) a Black African or other person with dark skin
Word Origin
C16: see Black, Moor
Collins English Dictionary - Complete & Unabridged 2012 Digital Edition
© William Collins Sons & Co. Ltd. 1979, 1986 © HarperCollins Publishers 1998, 2000, 2003, 2005, 2006, 2007, 2009, 2012
Cite This Source

American Psychological Association (APA):
blackamoor. (n.d.). *Dictionary.com Unabridged*. Retrieved March 09, 2016 from Dictionary.com website http://www.dictionary.com/browse/blackamoor
Chicago Manual Style (CMS):
blackamoor. Dictionary.com. *Dictionary.com Unabridged*. Random House, Inc. http://www.dictionary.com/browse/blackamoor (accessed: March 09, 2016).
Modern Language Association (MLA):
"blackamoor". *Dictionary.com Unabridged*. Random House, Inc. 09 Mar. 2016. <Dictionary.com http://www.dictionary.com/browse/blackamoor>.
Institute of Electrical and Electronics Engineers (IEEE):
Dictionary.com "blackamoor," in *Dictionary.com Unabridged*. Source location: Random House, Inc. http://www.dictionary.com/browse/blackamoor. Available: http://www.dictionary.com/. Accessed: March 09, 2016.
BibTeX Bibliography Style (BibTeX)
@article {Dictionary.com2016,
   title = {Dictionary.com Unabridged},
   month = {Mar},
   day = {09},
   year = {2016},

url = {http://www.dictionary.com/browse/blackamoor},

(4) "In a momentous event in the history of African Diaspora visual culture studies, more than 200 scholars, curators, independent writers, artists, photographers and other arts professionals from the African Diaspora are gathering to make presentations at the *Black Portraiture[s] II: Imaging the Black Body and Re-Staging Histories* conference in Florence Italy, May 28-May 31, 2015. Their audience will include numerous other scholars, museum professionals and artists. The conference is sponsored by New York University in association with the Hutchins Center for African and African American Research at Harvard University." The International Review of African American Art Plus, Extending the Coverage of the Print Journal

(5) see "The Moabite Key," The Key to Understanding Kemetic, Hebrew and Moabite Script. Min. Cozmo El

"THE KEY TO UNLOCKING THE WISDOM OF THE ANCIENT ONES! The ancient Moabite script owes much of it's origin to the upper Kemetic script known as Sinatic script. In fact, the arrangement, inherent meanings of Moabite letters and numeric values are all owed to this script dismissed by most of the Afro-Centric circles as Semetic. As a result much of the precious knowledge and wisdom preserved by our ancient forefathers has gone unclaimed by those whom it was preserved for. However, upon further study, one may begin to realize that there is a storehouse of knowledge and wisdom in the descendant languages of the Kemet. Use this Key to unlock the mysteries of the east. OVER 100 SIGNS AND SYMBOLS INSIDE!!!" http://www.amazon.com/The-Moabite-Key-Introduction-Phenomenological/dp/1514396939

*black (n.)
Old English blæc "the color black," also "ink," from noun use of black (adj.). From late 14c. as "dark spot in the pupil of the eye." The meaning "black person,

African" is from 1620s (perhaps late 13c., and blackamoor is from 1540s). To be in the black (1922) is from the accounting practice of recording credits and balances in black ink.

Made in United States
Troutdale, OR
08/15/2024